POEMS

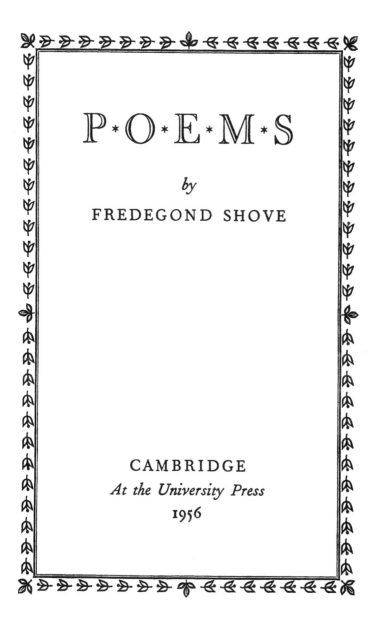

P·O·E·M·S

by

FREDEGOND SHOVE

CAMBRIDGE

At the University Press

1956

CAMBRIDGE
UNIVERSITY PRESS

University Printing House, Cambridge CB2 8BS, United Kingdom

Cambridge University Press is part of the University of Cambridge.

It furthers the University's mission by disseminating knowledge in the pursuit of education, learning and research at the highest international levels of excellence.

www.cambridge.org
Information on this title: www.cambridge.org/9781107544697

© Cambridge University Press 1956

First published 1956
First paperback edition 2015

A catalogue record for this publication is available from the British Library

ISBN 978-1-107-54469-7 Paperback

Cambridge University Press has no responsibility for the persistence or accuracy of URLs for external or third-party internet websites referred to in this publication, and does not guarantee that any content on such websites is, or will remain, accurate or appropriate.

CONTENTS

v

* From *Dreams and Journeys*
† From *Daybreak*

FREDEGOND SHOVE

Fredegond Shove was a daughter of Frederic William Maitland, Downing Professor of the Laws of England. During the 1914 war she married Gerald Shove, later a fellow of King's College, Cambridge. She lived in Cambridge for the greater part of her life and died there on 5 September 1949, about two years after the death of her husband.

Her published works were:

> *Dreams and Journeys* (Blackwell, 1918).
> *Daybreak* (The Hogarth Press, 1922).
> *Christina Rossetti* (Cambridge University
>   Press, 1931).

After her death a book called *Fredegond and Gerald Shove* was privately printed. It contained her memoir of Gerald—a memoir full of the happiness of their life together, and some recollections of her own childhood and upgrowing. She told of her earliest sense of 'the Almighty's sheltering roof tree', of the fear that came to her as she viewed the evil of this 'secondary world'. 'I was shocked and sickened at the ways of one world, whilst I clung, ever more secretly, to the faint legacy which the other had left me.' She told also of that day when at the age of fourteen 'in the charity of the brown autumn sunlight, I felt myself to be one of those who must try to relate their experiences, and to whom experiences are scenes, colours and sounds always, rather than events or actions.'

The poems in this book have been chosen from her unpublished as well as from her published work. Selection has not been easy owing to the large number of unpublished poems, the need for brevity, the various appreciations of those who have so kindly read through Fredegond's manuscripts, and my own unpractised discernments. Very few of the unpublished poems are dated but, viewing the whole of her work, one can trace the putting off of Bloomsbury, the putting on of Catholicism, the growing ardour of her love for animals, her deepening fears. In the main, however, time did not alter the experiences she wished to describe, nor her telling.

My cousin Miss Mary Fisher [Mrs Bennett] is joint owner of Fredegond's manuscripts, and I acknowledge with gratitude her permission to publish, and her help in selection.

I may, perhaps, be forgiven for saying that the surname Shove rhymes with mauve.

ERMENGARD MAITLAND

viii

THE POEMS

A DREAM IN EARLY SPRING

Now when I sleep the thrush breaks through my dreams
With sharp reminders of the coming day:
After his call, one minute I remain
Unwaked, and on the darkness which is Me
There springs the image of a daffodil,
Growing upon a grassy bank alone,
And seeming with great joy his bell to fill
With drops of golden dew, which on the lawn
He shakes again, where they lie bright and chill.

His head is drooped; the shrouded winds that sing
Bend him which way they will: never on earth
Was there before so beautiful a ghost;
Alas! he had a less than flower-birth,
And like a ghost indeed must shortly glide
From all but the sad cells of memory,
Where he will linger, an imprisoned beam,
Or fallen shadow of the golden world,
Long after this and many another dream.

LITURGY

I

O deliver me, deliver me from my own self,
    From treachery, from fear, from hate;
It seems so long that I have been laid up on the shelf
Like a broken cup or a too, too brittle plate;
    Take me, O take me; wash me with your beams;
        O good Lord, deliver me,
Deliver me from the horror and from the dishonour of my
        dreams;
    Set me free.

II

At Easter Christ rose up out of the sepulchre and from the
        sheet,
    From bitterness, from hate, from death;
He rose as an example of the assured, the fleet,
The strong and the possessor and the stainless faith.
    Show us, O show us how the earth bore that flight;
        O deliver us from this—
From the tumult, the battle, from the axe and from the night;
    Gloria in excelsis.

III

Deliver us and exalt us in the teeth of the gale,
    From the galleys of time, the loom and from the yarn
Whereof our fear is spun, and from the forge and the flail,
And from the stable, the ship and the barn.

Free us as you have freed the frail sisterhood
Of the windflowers where they spin their white sheaves
  In the labyrinths of the forest
  And in the lightening of the wood;—
    Make us as the leaves,—

IV

Praising and singing when the life and when the peace
  Are begun in those nests where the eggs are laid low
And the cocks strut abroad and the rain comes without cease
    Making the grass grow:
Acting and desiring as the sower and as the plough
Going forth under the great, bare ribs of the sky;
Give us the life after death, Lord, now, even now,
    And the voice to cry:

V

'O deliver me, deliver me, from evil and sin
From scorn, from absence, from hate and from lust
And give me the robe wherewith to come proudly in,
  Not weeping with moth, not creeping with rust,
But confident, but splendid,—quicken'd after the shower
Like to a pear tree that is green with all the white:
  O Lord, render my heart a fruitful bower
    For thy delight.

VI

Deliver me, deliver me; for my flesh is of the stuff
Of labour, of heaviness, of doubt and of care;
    But I have grieved and I have languished
    And O I have been punished enough;
        Why should I despair?
Take me, then, take me from the halter and from the hook,
    Bury my sorrow,
Bury my shadow and my false likeness in the brook;
    Give me to-morrow.

VII

Wherefore, I beseech you that are the beginning and the end,
    Show me thy splendour in the appearance of its shape
And come to me at my calling by the wicket like a friend,
    Giving me the vision which is the only escape;
Not that I may maunder and may wonder and may dream
    But that I may give clothing and food,
Beauty to my descendants and water to my team,
    In the name of all good.'

4

SNOWDROPS

'When did you first see snowdrops?'
  'The day that I was born,
With candles by the cradle
  And frost upon the lawn,
Icicles on the laurels
  And nothing yet begun
Except the march of snowdrops
  Behind the winter sun.'

UPSTAIRS

No one can follow me
    Upstairs,
Up my shady stairs, my stairs of cedar wood,
    My polished stairs
Leading to the attic,
    Neighbour to the stars.
No one can follow me
    Into my dreams,
My meditations, the refuges which my hunger finds for me:
    Holes amid the clouds,
Shelter among the tangled howling winds,
    Deserted hearths upon the stoop of the air.
Bits of broken plaster and the blessed skulls of angels,
Lonely forlorn dells amid the water-ways of space,
    Wayward bowers in the sunlight.
Freshness, forlornness, solitude, peace,
    The roof peaks of aerial cities,
Remote shores where the blazoning ether-waves
    Thunder, reverberate everlastingly
        Echoing Time.

Here I sit watching, here I lose touch with earth,
    And am born again amid the bodiless
Bells, and the shadows where souls are shaken
By eddies and gusts of invisible laughter.

And here the five senses that have shepherded
   My soul from the cradle,
And will soon propel her to the grave,
   Turn into five arrows of fire
Pointing intensely towards the zenith of my hopes, my
      dreams,
My first-born dreams, my fragile imaginings.
Here they bid me live as a wire does,
Stretched out taut against the sea of everlasting air
   Here they bid me ponder.

Now the voice of the city beneath me
Is blown forth and upward like a naked spire—
All the cries that are swept out of the sepulchre—
All the emanations of its human sadness—
Toil, machinery, domesticity and decay,
Are made vocal, are composed, and distilled and imprisoned
Into that one thin shoot of the spiral striking aloft
And trembling like a form from which the
Sheets of corruption
Have been silently and quickly withdrawn.

There it stands, the frail and guilty echo—
   The mortal voice that has discarded its mantle of soot—
It stands shaking in the amphitheatre of live space,
   Uttering its last long cry of dissolution and despair:
'Comfort, O comfort' it seems to cry

'Earth that is an outcast among the stars of heaven
Vexed close to the heart and foul in her grave—
    Her airy grave of wonders,
    Her deep bed of seas.
Give rest, give peace and the first pure glimmer of the
        planets—
Give tongues, the yellow harps of happiness, and joy, and
        harmony,
Give wings, the gay wings of spirit everlastingly dipped
In dappled rivers and in cold ponds
    And in spangled orchards.
Give melody, give fire, give youth, give colour
To the strayed sister, to the dying star, to Earth—
Give, give grace to the thirsty.'

'No one can follow me'
    Says the earth,
'When I have unhooked and disbanded my garments of clay,
When I have put off the loud apparent
    Mind and speech of the city,
And have risen in the hot clear, sapphire-coloured air
    To address myself to my Author
    And to receive my absolution.'

O I can hear it all very clearly—
    The Earth-Voice and the other voices of the unknown
        stars,

And the loud, rude bellowing of the gales
    Tearing the ship-shroud to tatters—
Then I am at one with the earth in my wishes,
And the vision which begot all harmonies, which are souls,
Looks at me nearly thro' a pane of glass,
    Looks deep into my crooked abysmal human soul,
Built and plaited like a basket made by the cunning of ages—
It looks, and before I have time to answer,
It is gone and I am alone: lonely as before.

SOPS OF LIGHT

Stop still on the stair,
  (Draw in your breath):
Love is the whole air,
  There is no death:
Set the jug aside
  For beams to fill:
Peace is the housetide;
  Then be still.

Let the window stand
  Open to tree;
Light is the whole land
  And the whole sea:
The clocks in the house chime
  On the day's steep;
But the soul knows no time
  Nor any sleep.

A SMALL CHINK

To some there stands an open door,
   Wide, full of light—
They enter in and know no more
   Of inward night.
To others comes a seeking ray
   Through a small chink—
The door will open wide one day
   Perhaps, they think.

HOOPS AT DUSK

The west is changing, green succeeds on gold,
White stars begin to mount the bitter air,
    Slow dusk is coming on,
    Its velvet petals close
About the dying gardens and the roofs
Of sleepy cottages, with ivied eaves.

    These dahlias feel the dusk,
    Michaelmas daisies blue,
And marigolds hang down their coronals,
Rich with the last rays of the dying sun
    That has withdrawn its soul
    From the world's hollow cup—
Leaving this upland village to the care
Of candles and of fragrant autumn winds.

But children are about;
They fill the air with screams,
And madly drive their iron hoops abroad—
The music of the hoops is wild as bells
    Sprinkled upon a storm,
  Or frantic as the tune
Of harp and pipe and concertina played
  In company by frenzied spirits were.

The common vales and hills
This elfin madness fills,
And scatters ringing splinters on the field
Among the breathing sheep in their dark fold;
And yet the sound is sweet,
As sweet as echoes are.

The sound is purer, keener, than we dream
The voices of the stars in spring to be,
Keener and merrier
Than tune of scythes by night,
Sharpened among the virgin moon-daisies
Amid the shadows of a waving field;
By its shrill alchemy
A ghost might well be called
Out of a stalk, and naked bid to weep
For hours on the still, forgetful grass;
Or the green fairies might
Transcend their hidden cells
To lean on mushrooms in a frozen trance,
Bewitched by the cold magic of these hoops.

And now the light is done—
Its apple-coloured hue
Has faded from the kingdom of the sky,
Also the flowers in the garden shed
Their white and scarlet sheaves
Before the rising wind;

Now children will be vanishing like moths,
Leaving a tide of echoes in their wake,
    And I shall dream all night
    Of tunes they played to me,
Of hills and valleys where the glow-worms wink
Among the serried shapes of the gay leaves;
    And I shall think on elves
    In their enchanted towns.

THE RAIN

I went out into the rain—
   There was no one in the road—
Down the straight suburban lane
   Went my soul; a heavy load
Was my body. Dark the trees
   Brought the first September rain
To my face, and to my knees
   From the grassy border. Pain
Was nothing, quiet naught
   Filled the empty common day
Which with lonely dusk was fraught.
   Dead the houses, dead the way
Leading to some further death,
   Further, quieter, deeper still,
When the sleeper shall draw breath
   As a train does on a hill,
     Then stand still.

I was tired with my walk,
   Tired with things meaningless,
With the painless weight—death's talk—
   Nothing leads to nothingness.
I was tired of my life
   With its work, and work, and work,
With its anxious inner strife,

With its fear that pain may lurk,
And its long pretence of right.

I was tired with my walk,
  And with all the beings cold,
Dumb and hard, and fierce and lone,
  Prowling past me through the mould,
And the meat upon my bone,
  Seeming hardly worth one groan—
I had listened to death's talk.

Now I heard no sweetness wild
  From the spacious boughs of love;
Now no autumn berried child
  Came with basket bearing dove;
Now no sunshine made of dust,
  Something subtly exquisite,
Now the dark leaves tarnished rust
  Seemed too rich to bear new light—
God's first child was tombed in lead.
  Could my faith be still respite
Now that I was nearly dead
  With this tiredness in my head?

On my knees—I know it well—
  God has died to save the soul.
This the quiet lane to hell
  May be trodden to its goal,

But if truth is in my mind
　Let me look into my breast
Where the cross is graven, limned
　By the one who knows me best.

In the dark and dreadful place
　I am treading where despair
Sits with awful hidden face.
　In her poisonous dank hair,
In the dreadful nothingness,
　Is the hill of anguish raised,
And amid the horror's press
　Jesus pierced, and Jesus praised
Who can save from all distress.

Life came back into my brain
　When his dark and jewel sweet,
Holy, precious, dim with pain,
　Sacred face with pity's rain
Through the shadows seemed to fleet—
　Seemed to bend and bow again,
Seemed to smile and to repeat
　Something like a short refrain—
O so quiet, O so sweet
　On my spirit sprent the rain:
'But believe and thou shalt see,
　See and thou shalt live again,

But of spirit and of this
   Water sweet thou now dost kiss,
As it falls so straight on thee,
   Thou must first be born again.'
Miserere cried the tree.
   Deo gratias cried the rain.

THE HOUSE OF LIGHTS

The doors of Heaven stand ajar,
    Each portal opens on a star:
And as into that house I gaze
  I see the palace all ablaze
  With fiery torches, living, bright,
  With glory quenchless, ageless, white;
Transfixed at Heaven's flames I stand
    And quite forget that twilit land,
That lonely beach, that stormy sea,
  Those dark discernments which are me,
For, O, my Father's house doth shine
    With streams of beauty crystalline!

REVELATION

Near as my hand
The transformation: (time to understand
Is long, but never far,
As things desired are:)
No iceberg floating at the pole; no mark
Of glittering, perfect consciousness, nor dark
And mystic root of riddles; death nor birth,—
Except of heart, when flesh is changed from earth
To heaven involved in it: not at all strange,
Not set beyond the common, human range;
Possible in the steep, quotidian stream,
Possible in a dream;
Achieved when all the energies are still,—
Especially the will.

THE WATER MILL

There is a mill, an ancient one,
Brown with rain, and dry with sun,
The miller's house is joined with it
And in July the swallows flit
To and fro, in and out,
Round the windows, all about;
The mill wheel whirrs and the waters roar
Out of the dark arch by the door,
The willows toss their silver heads,
And the phloxes in the miller's beds
    Turn red, turn gray,
    With the time of day,
And smell sweet in the rain, then die away.
The miller's cat is a tabby, she
Is as lean as a healthy cat can be,
She plays in the loft, where the sunbeams stroke
The sacks fat backs, and beetles choke
In the floury dust. The wheel goes round
And the miller's wife sleeps fast and sound.
There is a clock inside the house,
Very tall, and very bright,
It strikes the hour when shadows drowse,
Or showers make the windows white;
Loud and sweet, in rain and sun,
The clock strikes, and the work is done.

The miller's wife and his eldest girl
Clean and cook, while the mill wheels whirl.
The children take their meat to school
And at dusk they play by the twilit pool;
    Bare-foot, bare-head,
    Till the day is dead,
And their mother calls them in to bed.
The supper stands on the clean-scrubbed board,
And the miller drinks like a thirsty lord;
The young men come for his daughter's sake,
But she never knows which one to take:
She drives her needle, and pins her stuff,
While the moon shines gold, and the lamp shines buff.

THE DARNED FROCK

My soul is tired of her dull darned frock
    And very weary of the work in house;
Is sick for dreams and countries where dreams flock
    Their silver breasts, and cries to pierce the close
Of heavy greenness. Now she woos the clock—
    That small shrined spirit—now invites the mouse,
The linnet's wings of dawn, the true dusk's rose,
The ghosts of mignonette, and pink, and stock,
As though some secret they might swift unlock.

And often in her shrinking from disdain,
    Differing dusts, and printed words, and pence—
And often in the sweetness born of rain,
    That hush that is a heart with no defence—
    She comes in sight of beauty's face intense,
And knows that sight may never come again.

The apple trees are green with fruit,
    In every rut blue thistles bloom,
And slowly, since the days are wet,
    The corn gets ripe and burns the gloom
Of darker fields; the blackberries
    Look coral pink along the hedge,
The gardens blaze with sunflowers,
    The ponds are covered with green sedge;
It rains and rains: the little ducks,
    That have no feathers yet but fluff,
Go paddling with their springtime cries
    From pool to pool, content enough;
The strong black pigs enjoy their grass,
    The children play till dusk comes on
Beset with storms; and so we pass
    Day after day: the hollyhocks
Are mere brown paper since the rain;
    The farmers grumble in their carts:
When will the sun come back again?
    A little elfin boy I know,
That plays in nettles all day long,
    Does not remember sunny days
And sings a never-ending song
    About the dappled cows at dusk,
The happy ducks and ruined plums;

He sings this song to every one
That passes by, and sometimes comes,
   Bringing a bunch of purple-heads,
To the back door for bread and tea:
   How pale he is, how paper-frail!
His arms are piteous things to see;
   He knows each passing tramp by name
And tells the stories of their lives—

   A long procession of despair,—
Mad boys, wild men and jealous wives,
   They travel in his childish brain
With shocking stealth, by secret means:
   His mother hears him moan at night
The names of ancient gipsy queens,

   Horse-dealers, quacks, and foreign youths
With monkey-jacks, of idiot churls,
   Of misers draped in beggars' gowns,
And odd, untidy harlot-girls;
   Their music and the farthing dips
By which they light their creaking souls

   Along the staircase of his thoughts
Disturb his slumber where he rolls
   Between the sheets,—a child of six
With touseled hair and twisted brain:
   'Oh dear,' he murmurs to himself,
'When will the angels come again?

   They came one night, with pipes and drums;

They were a silver band of joys,
    Red cheeks they had and silver wings
And trumpets fit for princely boys;
    They sang and harped and played all night;
The stars came floating in to hear,
    And all this cobweb-crowd of tramps
Began to waste and disappear.—

    White apples hang upon that tree
Outside my room, they'll soon be pink:
    It must be nearly morning now:
The stars are out.   It's fine I think.'

A WOOD CUTTER'S SONG

A child has eyes like dewberries; a child has cheeks like
   flame;
A child feels sudden love and hate, and sudden fear and
   shame.
I was a child when to the woods out of the womb I came.
The woods have aged, and so have I: I am as old as care;
My spirit is as dry as crust, my heart is cold and bare:—
Yet have I still a child's light laugh and still a child's strange
   stare.

FANCIES

In the fair willow tree
  Is a dark hollow:
When the spring twilight falls
  Light as a swallow,
Woodman and woodman's child
  Come to the river,
Dipping their pitchers down
  While the leaves quiver.

Sometimes the little girl
  After him lingers
Where the long branches dip
  Down glassy fingers;
But if she hears a wing
  Stir in the hollow
After her father she
  Flies like a swallow:
Witch in the willow tree,
  Have you bright glances?
Child of the woodcutter,
  Have you strange fancies?

FEBRUARY NIGHT

Hush my angel in the tree.
   The guinea-fowl has gone to roost
Sleep is sent to her and thee
   While the four winds just unloosed
Twist the tender chimney round,
Round, and round, and round.

Sleep my teardrop, sleep my sweet,
   February guards the stars,
Faintly, faintly falls their heat
   Out upon those cloudy bars.
In deep dreams the farms around
Are bound, and bound, and bound.

Rest my spirit in your cot,
   The fire trickles through the grate,
Still the ashes will be hot
   When you wake, however late.
But with sunbeams sweetly found
You shall be crowned, and crowned, and crowned.

I DREAMT I CLIMBED THE APPLE TREE

I dreamt I climbed the apple tree
And plucked the golden stars for thee;
I gave thee all the skies did hold
And thou wert dazzled with the gold,
I gave thee all the silver spires,
The crowns and triangles and fires,
The comets with their burning tails
And fragments shivered by the gales;
And easily they came to me
In the wide bosomed apple tree,
And easily my prize was given,
The heart of all that honeyed heaven.
Such futile things are dreams that shake
All time and space, and seem to make
A nonsense rhyme of all we learn
In the lean daylight when we yearn
For wonders. Yet those dreams of ours
Give us strange joys like midnight flowers;
And I to thee, if I can give,
Will all those beams by which I live
Most meekly offer, since it seems
That thou and I are bound in dreams.

EVERYONE HAS GONE TO TOWN

My house stands empty in the rain
   Everyone has gone to town.
They would not heed the weather-vane
   That dream of shops and buses brown,
And smuts, and lamps, and city streets,
And petrol, and rich meats.

My garden was too sweet to leave,
   So in the wet I dig and plant.
The fine acacias seem to grieve
   The rosemary is full of want,
The green and scented rustling things
Water my heart's dry springs.

But from the empty house I hear
   The old clock chime and he's alone,
For him the shades have come too near,
   What solitude is in his tone.
The windows tremble like the strings
Of a bruised harp, poor tender things.

And in the hall I know so well
   The little gloomy patterns race
And chase each other, I can tell,
   How coldly on the sunless place;
And damp and still, and lifeless airs
Play up and down the shabby stairs.

It will not do, I must go in
　　And change my shoes and wash my hands.
Upon the threshold—O my sin—
　　Did I forget her? There she stands
With tail upraised and blazing eyes
And arching back, and many cries.

She had been all alone since two
　　O'clock had struck—my little cat,
My Cuckoo, O my Cockatoo,
　　My small, my sweet, my fine, my fat,
My darling, O my first delight,
My wanton, wishful, fishful, sprite.

Then quickly to the larder she,
　　And I as she, together fly;
Upon the jug of cream do we
　　Together, with a great outcry,
Precipitate ourselves, and on
The plate of cod as white as snow.

And while I drink my early cup
　　Of china tea, she tears her fish;
And whilst I wash my tea things up
　　She rattles at her empty dish:
And O, how joyously the clock
Ticks off the minutes as they flock.

And O how joyfully it booms
    The hour of six when she has done.
Goodbye to gleams, and ghosts, and glooms,
    The rain has stopped, the yellow sun
Salutes the smoky, sooty train
That stands perspiring in the plain.

Then back they come, her master first,
    And afterwards her useful maid—
The one consumed with deathly thirst,
    The other in new shoes arrayed.
And to them both she runs and mews,
And gives to both of them their dues.

Meanwhile the rosemary and thyme,
    The luscious branched acacia trees,
The honeysuckle where she climbs,
    The pinks, the roses, and sweet-peas,
The wall-flowers and the pansies pied
Have been appeased, and satisfied.

BETTINA AT DUSK

The little tabby cat with wild white face
    Sits on the step, and peers into the pale
Shell-tinted twilight of a winter day.
    She knows each scent of spring in the warm gale,
She watches each dark spray.
    Her small warm body still, instinct with grace,
Sits calm—removed from play;
    And now the first green star swims in the swale,
And her green eyes behold it, far away.

From THE SOUTH WIND

The South Wind ruffles the great dark cat's hair
   As he sits on the wall himself to preen
His white heart-face is lifted pure and clear
   And his heart is happy, tuneful and serene.

A DREAM

I dreamt a tortoise crept into my care,
    Sensitive in his plaid shawl of bright shell;
I cherished him, but chanced to look elsewhere
    And gone was my new fondling,—peace as well.
I ran, I called, asked spirits, had no rest
    Until a voice declared
'He is not gone, his maker loved him best
    And you were unprepared.'

THE KINGDOM OF HEAVEN

Thou liest within me as a shell
   Lies in a pool,
Or as milk-wort were in Hell,
   So fresh, so cool—
Or as an icicle all clear
   And straight within—
Mirror of holiness and sheer
   Contempt of sin.
And round about thee I have built
   A fortress-yard,
A castle whose thick walls are guilt,
   So proud, so hard;
And many chambers where I walk
   So hard, so proud,
And many parlours where I talk
   So much, so loud.
But when these crumble in Hell's flame,
   So swift, so strong,
There will be left my heart, the same,
   My heart, a song;
I shall be gone and all my deeds,
   Myself—my year,
My hates, my angers and their seeds
   Will disappear.

Thou liest within the storm and art
   So safe, so still,
O Jesus of the human heart,
   Whom none can kill.

THE NEW GHOST

(And he casting away his garment rose and came to Jesus.)

And he cast it down, down, on the green grass,
Over the young crocuses, where the dew was—
He cast the garment of his flesh that was full of death,
And like a sword his spirit showed out of the cold sheath.

He went a pace or two, he went to meet his Lord,
And, as I said, his spirit looked like a clean sword,
And seeing him the naked trees began shivering,
And all the birds cried out aloud as it were late spring.

And the Lord came on, He came down, and saw
That a soul was waiting there for Him, one without flaw,
And they embraced in the churchyard where the robins play,
And the daffodils hang down their heads, as they burn away.

The Lord held his head fast, and you could see
That He kissed the unsheathed ghost that was gone free—
As a hot sun, on a March day, kisses the cold ground;
And the spirit answered, for he knew well that his peace was
    found.

The spirit trembled, and sprang up at the Lord's word—
As on a wild, April day, springs a small bird—

So the ghost's feet lifting him up, he kissed the Lord's cheek,
And for the greatness of their love neither of them could
  speak.

But the Lord went then, to show him the way,
Over the young crocuses, under the green may
That was not quite in flower yet—to a far-distant land;
And the ghost followed, like a naked cloud holding the sun's
  hand.

AVE MARIA

Ave Maria, sang the sea,
And brought the small white stars to me;
As pale and cold as seeds they lay
Among the strand of Milky-Way.
  Ave Maria, sang each star
  In secret where all secrets are.

Ave Maria, sang the wood
Where all the pines in conclave stood;
With recollection deep and dim
They breathed aloft their Vesper hymn,
  Ave Maria, sang each bough;
  And all the world was kneeling now.

MAY MORNING

Through the fair first flowers
   Went the Son of God,
Through the fields at sunrise
   Walked the King unshod,
In the long sweet grasses
   That were ripe for hay,
On a milk-warm morning
   Of joyful May.

There was still no scythesman
   In the meadows wide,
But there called a cuckoo
   Upon every side,
And there sang a blackbird
   In the wych-elm green.
Thus of birds in bowers
   Was the wonder seen

That the King Of Heaven
   Was to earth come down
Without sword or sceptre,
   Without pride or crown,
To walk through the grasses
   At the start of day,
In the sweet mild weather
   That is born of May.

AT NIGHT

A bell was swinging in my soul
　　Last night, all night.
A solemn tongue it had to toll,
Hung in a big and brazen bowl,
And slow and strange till morning came
Between the shutters with her light
The bell did ring, did swing, did sing,
　　All night, last night.

A bird kept flying thro' my soul
　　All night, last night,
She fluttered like a spring-tide flame,
And trembled like a drop of light.
The bird did shake, did wake, did quake
　　All night, last night.

A face was bending over me
　　At morn, at morn:
A face I could not rightly see,
But yet I knew that it was he,
And in my soul I said his Name
And a new love in me was born,
A love as free as wind in tree—
　　The love I bore my Enemy
　　　That night, last night.

And when my Enemy was Friend,
    In joy I woke.
All silence was: His face did bend
No longer, but these words he spoke:
'Pray for this Enemy of thine
As I prayed long ago for mine
    One night, all night.'

DECEMBER MOON

More like some precious glass
　　Than pearl, the wide
And shallow steps to her December throne
So lately risen and so royally skied,
　　So sweetly un-alone,
Being still half sheeted by the smoky day,
And wintry primrose light of sunken sun,
Being still so near the stooping branches gray
　　And steeples, so at one
With earth's half glory and the sighs which pass
Across the stubborn stiff, frost-bitten grass;
　　How pure, how precious she—
And of all moons most sweet.

OUT OF DOORS

Out of doors it is so cold,
　　Still so wintry, still so pale,
Yet the aconites bring gold
　　Lamps to light the dusky veil
Of the evening mist which lies
In these withered shrubberies.

Out of doors it is so cold,
　　Still so sharp the wind brings tears,
Yet in the far wintry fold
　　Lambs are born—and each one bears
Her small spring as might a tree
Show one bud, and laugh with glee.

Out of doors it is, O chill—
　　Bitter draught of wind and keen,
Yet the snowdrops come and still,
　　Meek, transparent, white and green,
Stand to see the young moon born
In that sky the winds have shorn.

Out of doors I feel the Spring
　　Creeping through the alleys dim,
For I see the young Moon's ring,
　　And I hear the faint ewe's hymn,
And I stoop to pluck these flowers
Which have braved the world's wild powers.

THE WATERING POT

Geraniums red, sweet leaved, are dry,
For water all the blossoms cry;
Rich Marigolds and Lilies droop,
The Roses fade, the clustered group
Of Canterbury Bells is sighing—
Heaven sends no cloud to wash the dying:
Therefore the water-can must shake
Thin sprays, and tiny rainbows break
On every bough, and bud and bell,
With tinkling sound, and who can tell
What sweetness may not shining spring
To fill the spray, while Blackbirds sing,
And down behind the shivering trees
The sun goes trembling in the breeze?

From THE RIVER OF LIFE

Far away and far away
Flows the river of pure Day;
Cold and sweet the river runs
Through a thousand, thousand suns;
Washed and gold and trancéd clear
Flows the river free from fear,
From the throne of all Delight,
From the crystal casket bright,
Down into our dusky vale
Where the April willows pale
Grieve and ever grieve again
In the city of our pain.

Through the murk and through the flame,
Through the rocks whence sorrow came,
Flows the river, sweet of birth,
Washing this untender earth.

THE BATHE

There is the pale blue sea at last—
   So longed for, dreamed of. Now set free
I run across the spacious sand
   And throw myself inside that sea:
O coldness more desired than sweet
   Spills of sunshine, cold that keeps
A wondrous jewelled froth of heat,
   Refreshment, joy, and ease from deeps
Deep drawn that none may understand:
   Now no more quite earth—no more
So chained, so dry, so sore, so quick
To feel each tiny dusty prick
   Of cruel toil; no longer sore
Or even separate. I ride
Out, out on the outgoing tide
   I flow, I sink, I swim, I soar—
Translated and beatified.

Now have we no more need of words
   Rhythms or rhymes or runes or tunes.
I lift my face to the pale sky,
   I gaze and in the gulls ringed up
Read the strange riddle of the birds
   Whose life is here upon the dunes
Yet on the wave's crest equally.

No need to think, to know, to ache;
    No need to look beyond or back,
    My present need is all, I rest
    Upon the swell, and the foam's crest,
And my limbs the present break,
What is not here I do not lack.
    O loveliness so cold, so sweet,
    Trimmed coldness with thy hidden heat,
Blue loveliness wide, wide awake.

The shore looks dreamlike from the sea,
    The sea looks dreamlike from the shore,
    The heavens to both divine and light.
Now all is over suddenly—
    The bathe that is my day's delight—
But I am glad, content to be:
    Dear summertime, dear shore, goodnight.

MORE TUNES IN MY SPIRIT BLOW

Break, O break my heart-sweet song
Of green boughs in the burning day;
Then let the music that too long
In me has troubled thought away
    To pour, to flow,
    Like melted snow;
To waste, to shimmer in the air,
That I can freely, freely share—
For more tunes in my spirit blow
  From God, than I can bear.

For EU product safety concerns, contact us at Calle de José Abascal, 56–1°, 28003 Madrid, Spain or eugpsr@cambridge.org.

www.ingramcontent.com/pod-product-compliance
Ingram Content Group UK Ltd.
Pitfield, Milton Keynes, MK11 3LW, UK
UKHW030913160425
457438UK00001B/1